A sibling For Our Oldest

Musings on the Triplet Experience

Rob Murphy

REMIII

REMIII

To Anna
For making this life and book possible - it was a lot of fun!

Contents

Introduction

In the adoption community, the day a family gets their new child is called "gotcha day." We already had four children, including a set of five-year-old triplets, but despite that, today was a gotcha day for our family. We were all packed into the family car and on our way to Detroit Metropolitan Airport to pick up the 3-month-old Korean boy we had just adopted.

We were all very excited to meet our new family member, and so arrived early and nervously waited. Soon they announced the arrival of the plane from Korea, and a short time later, a long line of people started to exit the aircraft. A short while later, the child escorts emerged, pushing a stroller containing our smiling baby boy. With no fanfare, they asked if we were the Murphys and then simply handed the baby over to my wife. We all gathered around and made a great fuss over him before heading home to begin life with our fifth child.

Years later, it occurred to me that none of our children had ever asked where babies come from because they knew that when a family wants a baby, they simply go to the airport and pick one up. Every family has stories that remind its members why they are essential to one another and serve as the glue that binds them.

My initial instinct in recording these stories was therapeutic, a way to survive and comprehend the chaos that is a triplet household. Years later, when the chaos became mundane, I continued to write so that one day my children could hear the stories of the path we took to get them here.

A Sibling for Our Oldest

Musings on the Triplets Experience

Rob Murphy

The Lottery, Meteorites, and Shark Bites

∞∞∞

February 11, 1998, 11:00 p.m. Today we had triplets! Our triplets were born today! Today I got to watch triplets being born! Wow! Let's see. Bought groceries, washed the car, did the laundry, mowed the lawn, and had triplets. Pretty normal to-do list except that last item. Triplets! Wow! What an amazing thing to be able to say. Think of the implications. How many people get to say that? I won the lottery! I got hit by a meteorite! I got bit by a shark! I had triplets. You gotta admit—it's not something you hear every day.

Yes, today was quite a day. We knew today was the day it was going to happen, but how can you prepare for watching your wife give birth to three babies and lose sixty pounds in two minutes? Even though I was prepared by agonizing months of waiting, once it starts to happen, no amount of preparation can equip you for this kind of thing. I'm sure I sound like any other father babbling on about the birth of his children and how amazing it is, but we're talking about triplets here! This ain't no little thing here! It's three of 'em! It's triplets!

I must start by saying that I never actually thought this day would really come. Understand that I had read as much on the subject of multiple births as I possibly could find. The more I read, the more it became clear that triplets are an incredible long shot. In 1998, in the entire country, there were only something like

250 sets of triplets born out of the millions of births. Of those 250 sets, only a little more than half were born complete, alive, and healthy. Sadly, of those that did make it home, an even smaller number of triplet sets made it through the first year with all babies still alive. Getting pregnant with triplets is entirely reasonable but actually taking three healthy little creatures home is quite another realm entirely.

We were hoping for another child. By that I mean a singular child, one, an individual. The goal was one more baby, and even in my wildest thoughts, a solitary, unaccompanied, acapella—an all by itself—single baby was what we wanted. Had I known, well, I never would have been able to muster the proper glint in my eye to inspire the production of such a blessed event. Still, we wanted a sibling for our oldest, so what's one more child, right?

Anna's pregnancy can only be compassionately described as challenging. By the end of Anna's first month, before the pregnancy was even confirmed by medical tests, Anna was already having severe morning sickness. By severe, I mean torturous. She was entirely overwhelmed by nausea—nausea so complete and all-consuming that, when it was interrupted by violent periods of vomiting, it appeared to be a relief to her. A short while later, her doctor confirmed that a little bundle of joy was on its way. Obviously, we couldn't have been happier, although since Anna was green, vomiting, and face down in a toilet when she found out, it was hard to tell she was pleased about it. Finding out we were pregnant was probably the highlight of the pregnancy, other than the actual birth.

The cause of all of Anna's extreme nausea was something called hyperstimulation. Apparently, when a woman is pregnant, her ovaries secrete fluids into the abdominal cavity. In something like 99.9 percent of all pregnancies, the amount of fluid is small, it is easily absorbed by the body, and it doesn't cause even a slight discomfort. The other .01 percent of the time, the ovaries secrete vast amounts of fluid. In fact, they secrete far more fluid than any ten bodies could ever absorb. If the body cannot process this fluid, it has to go somewhere, but the way the body is organized, there is no place for this fluid to go. So, it accumulates and accumulates and accumulates until pretty soon you look like you're eight months pregnant—at one month. We discovered the joys of hyperstimulation when I noticed that Anna had gained what looked to be about twenty-five pounds in a single weekend. Concerned, we called her doctor, who told us she needed to see Anna immediately.

Hyperstimulation is cured naturally by the body, but the process takes time. During that time, the doctors were at a loss as to how best to treat her rapidly expanding girth. Endless testing produced a consensus that recommended draining her every couple of days. That involved a foot-long needle and a syringe the size of a turkey baster! This needle had to be inserted into her abdomen, avoiding all organs and muscle groups, until it found the cavity where the fluid was building up. If they didn't hit any essential organs or muscle groups, they could suck out the excess liquid, and this relieved the pressure quite well. However, they always hit vital organs and muscle groups, so this was an incredibly painful procedure to endure every other day or so. Finally, one of the doctors decided that this was not solving the problem. He determined that the only way to fix this was to let the fluid build until it couldn't build any more—kind of like allowing a zit grow. After about a week of this, Anna was moved to cardiac intensive care because they were "concerned about heart failure." Her pulse was over 155 beats per minute, and her blood pressure went through the roof. Oh yeah. Her kidneys were failing too. Compared to all this, nausea didn't seem so bad.

After about four weeks in the hospital, Anna was ten weeks pregnant. At this point, the doctors decided to do the first ultrasound of the baby to find out how it was doing. I clearly remember sitting in the cold, dark ultrasound room, staring at the screen as the technician first checked the conditions of Anna's ovaries.

You could clearly see the cysts on them that were secreting all the fluid. Each ovary had several cysts randomly scattered along its surface, looking somewhat like the eyes on a potato. The technician noodled around with that view, then moved onto something else that also apparently had cysts on it. The technician calmly inspected each of these new cysts, looking at each one from a couple of different angles and magnifications.

Then, coldly and without inflection, as if he was ordering a cup of coffee, the ultrasound technician said, "Congratulations, you're having triplets." He then immediately left the room. After a long pause, I responded, "Thank you!" I then sat there stunned, holding my wife's hand, looking at those three tiny "cysts," realizing that life as I knew it would never be life "as I knew it" again.

Anna was home for a week when her second difficulty developed. For some reason, she started showing all of the symptoms of appendicitis. We rushed her to the emergency room, where over the next eleven hours, every possible intern, resident, nurse, and surgeon visited Anna. She came very close to becoming about the only woman to ever undergo an appendectomy while pregnant with triplets.

Doctors significant and not were lining up to witness and participate in the surgery. They did all manner of tests and ultrasounds, trying to be sure of the diagnosis. But there were so many babies blocking the view that doctors could not get an unobstructed look at the appendix. The room buzzed with excitement as they went about the business of preparing a triplet mom for an emergency appendectomy.

Finally, a senior doctor stepped in, stopping the madness by deciding to err on the side of the babies until they were sure. They never did find out what the problem was, and after a few days the symptoms subsided, so they simply sent her home.

At four months of pregnancy, Anna started to feel pretty good, and school was about to start, so she went back to work. Other than being more tired than usual, this went fine. Then one day, I got a call that Anna was in the emergency room. Apparently, she had lost vast amounts of blood all over the floor in the teachers' restroom at the high school where she worked. Someone called 911, and all kinds of emergency vehicles and personnel stormed the building.

The restroom was a tiny room, designed for one person at

a time. However, this limited square footage did not deter the local fire and rescue company from using all available means to do everything they could possibly do. It seems that they actually managed to pack as many as ten of these yahoos (plus my wife) into the room at one time. The discussions on treatment protocol ranged from CPR to brain surgery right there on the bathroom floor. Luckily, the ambulance driver was not part of this old-boy network and simply whisked her off to the hospital. At the same time, the hot dogs from the fire department were still trying to figure out how to get the ladder truck into the bathroom.

Anyway, the message that I got said to call the secretaries at the school to find out where they had taken my wife. I did this and was very clearly told that Anna had asked to be taken to William Beaumont Hospital in Royal Oak, Michigan. Anna had wanted to go to the other hospital because that was where her personal doctors practiced. I jumped in the car and raced forty-five minutes in rush hour traffic to the hospital. I parked and found the information desk and asked the lady behind the computer wherein the hospital I might find my wife. I supplied her with my wife's name, and she pecked at a few keys. She tapped some more and then did it again.

She then excused herself and returned a short while later with another woman who repeated the process. I asked if there was a problem and was told in a slightly concerned voice that they had no record of my wife being admitted to this hospital. Worried, I called my wife's best friend, who was with her, to find out what was going on. She explained that Anna had stabilized and that they were waiting for an ultrasound technician to take Anna to do a scan. I told her about the hospital not knowing where Anna was, and she quickly told me to come to the emergency room—that they were behind curtain seven. I said, "Great —I'll be there in a couple of minutes."

With that, I hung up and made my way to the emergency room. I entered, followed the signs, and quickly made my way to curtain seven. I entered and was surprised to see a large, old, bald black man sleeping soundly where my small, blonde, cranky wife was supposed to be. I slipped back out and sheepishly wandered over to the emergency room information desk. There I repeated the scene with another lady and another computer.

Concerned, I called her friend again to find out what was going on! She said, "Rob, I am standing by Anna's bed right now! We are behind curtain seven." I said, "Jackie, I am standing outside curtain seven, and there is an old, bald black man lying in that bed, and you are not next to him! There was a long pause. "Rob . . . what hospital are you at?

"William Beaumont! What hospital are you at?"

The drive to Huron Valley Hospital took about an hour. Apparently, the ambulance driver, whose wife had been through a similar ordeal, had learned that getting IVs started as soon as possible would go a long way toward saving the life of the babies. Knowing that, he convinced her en route that Huron Valley, being the closest hospital, offered the best chance of saving the babies' and that is all that mattered.

When I arrived at Huron Valley Hospital, they were prepping Anna for the ultrasound. I expected her to be a mental mess, given that I had been told that she had a miscarriage, but she was extraordinarily calm and composed. The ultrasound technician dimmed the lights and started the test. Anna squeezed my hand as the technician carefully hid the screen from our view. After just a few minutes, the technician suddenly turned the screen to us and said, "This is so exciting! I've never seen triplets still alive on an ultrasound. See: three little heartbeats."

There they were—those three little cysts again, this time much bigger and each with a clearly beating heart. Seeing this, Anna collapsed into the mess that I had expected to find in the first place. This, of course, totally baffled me, as I would have expected that finding them alive would be a joy to her. She later explained that it, indeed, was a joy, but given the amount of blood she had lost, she was sure that she had lost the babies. Finding out they were still there was just a totally unexpected joy for her.

None of the doctors could give us a definitive answer on why or where all the blood came from. But as long as it had stopped and the babies were still all kicking, we might as well go home. And so we did, armed with instructions for Anna to stay off her feet, drink lots of water, and see her specialists as soon as possible.

The next day we went to the high-risk pregnancy special-ist. This visit became the starting point for a brand-new adven-ture. He informed us that Anna's teaching career for the year was over and that Anna could now do anything else that she cared to —as long as she stayed flat on her back in bed while she did it. We were also told that he wanted to put Anna on a device that would monitor for small contractions. Its job was to warn us if she was going into early labor. That seemed to make sense to us, so we went home to begin my new life as a butler and Anna to start her new life as a potato.

The first day of life with this arrangement was pretty much what we both expected. She hated it, and so did I. However, the real hell began when the United Parcel Service delivered the con-traction monitoring device, or CMD. Now, the CMD looked in-nocuous enough. It was about the size of a cell phone and was held in place by a large Velcro belt that looked like an ACE bandage.

The idea was that, if the CMD was placed in the correct spot on the side of her growing stomach, it could "listen" for con-tractions that Anna couldn't even feel. It would listen for these micro contractions and then record how strong they were and how often they happened. This information could then be sent via phone line to a machine located in the doctor's office, and then the doctor could determine whether everything was OK or not. Contractions more often than every four minutes were a problem.

So far, this all sounded great to us. However, in practice, this CMD was as bad as any torment could be, and may very well have caused as many contractions as it monitored. Here's why. First, we understood the importance of monitoring, so we wanted to use it correctly. The placement of the CMD was critical. If not successfully placed, the CMD would give off an obnoxious alarm or screech like a giant bird being squeezed. This was obviously intended so that when it slipped out of place, you could just move it back in the correct spot. But there was no correct spot; the damned thing just screeched at us all of the time. We would continuously reposition the CMD until it quit screeching at us, then carefully secure it in place and hold our breath. Then without Anna having so much as blinked, the stupid thing would just start to screech at us again. After a few days, we were entirely frustrated by this silly thing that we were ready to feed it to the lawn mower. Actually, looking back, CMD's are very much like living with infant triplets. Had we had to live with it long enough, it would have been excellent training.

Fortunately, while the CMD annoyed the hell out of us, it ultimately did its job very well. After a few weeks, it began to pick up far more than eight contractions an hour. Finally, it became clear to the doctors that these contractions were indeed a sign of early labor. At this point, Anna was only eighteen weeks pregnant, and to be safe, they wanted to admit Anna to the hospital "for a while," until they got the contractions under control. We didn't know it at the time, but Anna would not come home again from the hospital until after the babies were born.

About six months into the pregnancy, Anna started having contractions at a rate that just couldn't be managed without some help. In response to this, they put her on something called magnesium sulfate. At least that's what they told us they were using it for. I don't believe it; I think it is used to torture pregnant ladies who complain too much while they are waiting for their babies to be born.

The doctors had warned us that if the contractions got too bad too early in the pregnancy, one of the best medicines to stop the contractions was magnesium sulfate. They warned us about magnesium sulfate specifically because, while it does its job wonderfully, it does have some uncomfortable side effects. "Uncomfortable" can't come close to describing the impact it had on Anna.

The "effects" started with just making her so dizzy that she didn't know who I was and progressed on past, making her so disoriented she did not know who she was either. However, the real threat of being "on" magnesium sulfate was that it made her throw up nonstop. A single dose of magnesium sulfate lasts about twenty hours. While it did indeed stop the contractions, Anna threw up for about twenty hours straight. I got to hold her hair. After a week of this, the medicine did its job, and the contractions settled down.

Anna's days in the hospital had become a constant search for a comfortable position to lie down. She had grown to over sixty inches in breadth, so for her to lay stomach down was not an option. On her back was equally unacceptable because the weight of the babies tended to push down on her lungs. This made breathing just about impossible, and laying on her sides did not work very well either. In that position, the babies tended to push down on her bladder, which at this point was always full and squished to one-quarter of its original size. Since no place was remotely comfortable, she tended to be in constant movement from one position to the next, kind of like a whale rolling in the surf. This painful ballet went on endlessly, interrupted by nurses every ten minutes telling her to drink more water. And every time she drank more water, the doctors immediately entered, wanting to press on her belly or check her cervix.

Drinking water was the nurses' solution to pretty much every complaint that Anna had. This, of course, compounded the squished bladder problem. We were continually told that the single most crucial thing Anna could do to prolong the pregnancy was to drink lots of water. In fact, Anna's water intake was strictly monitored, and it was prescribed that she drink literally gallons of water every single day. The thought was that large amounts of fluids were essential to keeping contractions to a minimum and thus prolonging the pregnancy. The longer the gestation, the healthier the babies. However, the more pregnant Anna got, the bigger she got, and the smaller her bladder was squished, making it harder to drink the prescribed amount of water.

However, Anna's biggest complaint the entire time was that she couldn't get any sleep. Nurses seemed to come in every twenty minutes to wake her up to see if she needed a sleeping pill. Then, every night at 4:00 a.m., the dutiful hospital custodial crew waxed and cleaned the floors with their big machines.

She had lots of roommates during her stay, one who had no less than fifteen family members in her room all day long. They cycled in and out, all close to labor and in pain. Pain is not a quiet thing, no matter how hard you try to ignore it.

But the people who disrupted her sleep the most were the three tiny neonates that would start to kick and twist each and every organ that they could get their hands on. Any time Anna accidentally found sleep or a way to get comfortable, the babies would kick it into high gear with a rousing game of organ volleyball.

The morning of the birth, I got to the hospital at 9:30 a.m. The doctors had scheduled a 1:00 p.m. cesarean delivery, and I wanted to get there in plenty of time. However, when I arrived, Anna was in more than a little pain. During her pregnancy, she had grown far beyond what you could possibly expect a human to withstand. Her regular twenty-eight-inch waist was now sixty-eight inches!

I stood by her bed, and as I did, I tried to remain calm. Still, now it was clear to me that the pain she was experiencing was far beyond the normal mind-numbing pain that had become her way of life for the last sixteen weeks. She was working very hard to breathe and struggling just to stay lucid. The nurses seemed incredibly unconcerned by her condition. As was their habit, they simply told Anna to drink more water.

For days, I had been warning the doctors that Anna could not take much more, that they needed to deliver the babies as soon as possible. The doctors, who I'm sure must know their trade, always responded to our insistence with apparent casual indifference to Anna's pain. They would say that the babies were only at twenty-eight weeks or thirty weeks or thirty-two weeks, and every day would make a big difference to the health of the babies. They would go on to say "let's just go one more week" as if they, too, somehow felt her pain and knew it wasn't that bad. Finally, after thirty-four long weeks of pregnancy, the doctors gave in and scheduled a cesarean section for that day at 1:00 p.m. Quite honestly, if they had not agreed at that very minute to schedule a delivery time, Anna was going to get up and walk out of the hospital and find some taxi driver to deliver those babies.

This day was different. On this day, there was a fear in Anna's eyes for the first time. When the doctor came in to talk with her about it (four hours late), the conversation was concise. I expected him to do some elaborate examination or ultrasound, at least. Instead, he came in, looked Anna in the eyes, and started to ask how she was doing. But before he even got the words out of his mouth, he interrupted himself and said, "Wow—you're ready!" Just like that! After weeks of begging, after weeks of elaborate tests and drinking barrels of water, he looks in her eyes and decides it's time. Any other response at that moment would have gotten him beaten up by a very cranky pregnant lady.

As I waited with Anna, it was clear that the scheduled time might not be soon enough. It was only 10:00 a.m., and she was in terrible pain, far worse than any pain I had seen her in before. The doctors had installed a catheter to prepare for surgery. It turns out that the babies were apparently doing quite well. They had discovered this catheter and decided that it was their first toy. In celebration of this gift, they were kicking at it, causing their mother an incredible amount of pain.

Contractions were by now only one minute apart and soaring off the intensity chart. Anna was clearly not going to make it to the scheduled delivery time. By now, she was more than willing to push those little people out without any help from the doctors or their painkillers. I have no doubt that she would have delivered them by herself had the babies cooperated. However, two of the babies were breech, which at this point, I'm sure she would have dealt with. However, the last baby was transverse or laying sideways over the only means of escape. Pushing a baby out in the breech or even normal position is heroic enough, but pushing a baby out sideways is well beyond the capacity of our species.

About 10:15, Anna's doctor came again just to check in

and make sure we were still on track for the 1:00 p.m. delivery. This doctor was clearly now in sync with Anna because, without speaking, they looked at each other for a few seconds. He gently reached up and touched her tummy—kind of like a cowboy scratching the back of his favorite horse. With that, he gave her a final pat and said, "Let me see if I can get things moving along sooner." He disappeared, leaving us alone.

As we held hands, I started to get very worried about my wife's long-term health for the first time. Fifteen minutes later, several medical types with a rolling bed came in. One said, "It's time to take you up." They loaded Anna, I gave her a kiss, and they took her away. I was left to pack up all of my wife's things and was told that someone would come to get me in a short while.

As I stuffed all the fragments of my wife's life into two small plastic garbage bags, it really started to hit me what was about to happen and what is essential in life. Among her belongings were a few books, some clothes, candy, and assorted toiletries. But the stuff that she obviously treasured during her sixteen-week hospital stay, her life-line if you will, were several small pictures of our three-year-old daughter, Kelsey[1], sixteen weeks of ultrasound pictures of the triplets, and her diary containing lists of baby names. All but a few were now crossed out.

A white coat then burst into the room with a blue plastic surgical gown and mask for me to put on and directed me to follow him. He introduced himself as the anesthesiologist and gave me a rundown about where I was supposed to sit and what I was supposed to do during the cesarean. He told me what to expect. We walked for what seemed like miles through a maze hallways and official-looking doors. When I was completely disoriented, he pointed to a simple black plastic chair, told me to sit, and said that someone would be out to get me in a minute. With that, he disappeared through two large swinging doors. As the doors swung open, I got a glimpse of a large crowd and bright lights. I sat alone with my thoughts in this empty hall for what was only a few seconds but seemed like hours.

But before the doors had actually stopped swinging, a nurse

burst through them and told me to follow her. She brought me into the operating room where Anna was already on the table, and the surgeons appeared to be well on their way into the operation. They sat me in a large high-backed stool next to Anna's head, and told me to stay put and hold Anna's hand. Several among the crowd of medical types came up to me individually and told me to speak up if I felt like I was going to faint or throw up.

I looked down at Anna, and she was smiling. This was a bright, unforced smile like I had not seen in weeks. Clearly, the anesthesiologist had done his job well. She spoke to me happily, but to be honest, she slurred so much I couldn't understand anything she said. I smiled, nodded back, and squeezed her hand.

The operating room was about thirty feet square and a hive of activity. In addition to the doctors we talked with every day, there appeared to be two other people holding knives and/or sticking their arms inside Anna's body. In addition to those two doctors at the operating table, there seemed to be at least eight different doctor-looking types gathered around watching. Circling these doctors was a score of nurses all busy with this or that. Off to my right was a well-behaved crowd of at least fifteen other people who also looked like doctors, each watching the goings-on intently. It turns out that they were all student doctors, and the birth of triplets was an exciting educational opportunity.

While I could not see directly into the surgical field, I had a pretty good view of a lot of things I'd only seen in books, except that when you see it in a book, it's not covered with blood. I was at the birth of our first child, so I had seen a cesarean-section birth before. Still, as I sat there watching, I was amazed at how big a cut they had to make to get the babies out. They use these sharp, tiny knives to create a chainsaw-size hole. I was even more amazed that they seemed confident they could get all of the "things" back where they belonged when they were done. Still, I kept thinking that a power outage at this moment would be an awful thing.

As the doctors methodically went about trying to get at the babies, one of them kept making a bad joke every few minutes. This went on for about fifteen minutes until, at 11:57 a.m., a nurse came over to me and asked if I had a camera, and I said yes. "You better get it ready," she said. With that, somebody held up a large mirror so my wife could see the action. Suddenly the surgeons started moving faster, and Anna let out a huge death gasp, tensed, shut her eyes, and squeezed my hand like she was trying to rip it off. I quickly scanned the room to see if anybody else was concerned and saw one of the doctors was pulling on two tiny blue-gray feet. Slowly the rest of the baby girl emerged. A nurse quickly grabbed the baby from the doctor and held her up for us to see. This was baby Claire, all five pounds eight ounces of her. As she floated there in the air, she calmly looked at us and was then quickly wrapped and whisked off to the baby's recovery room next door.

It turns out that Anna's large death gasp was nothing of the sort. Instead, Anna's lungs had been so squished for so long that when they took Claire out, there was suddenly room for her lungs to expand fully again. Anna gasped just because she had not been able to take a full breath in over sixteen weeks and was shocked by how it felt. As Claire left the room, the chief surgeon called over to the group of student doctors and asked if any of them had ever performed a breech delivery. None of them had, of course, so he said, "Well, come on over. We got enough here for everybody!" With that, three of them rushed over and excitedly stood behind him. It was now 11:58.

Almost immediately, a baby cried. I looked down at the surgical site, and one of the surgeon's arms seemed to be entirely inside of Anna. As he removed his arms, a baby boy emerged screaming bloody murder. They held him up for us to see as he screamed and screamed. Anna, by this point, was crying—she was so happy. I heard whispers from the crowd about how big and healthy the babies were. Nurses quickly took Quinn to the recovery room, and three more students hustled over as the others danced back into the crowd. Almost immediately, tiny little Emma had joined us. Emma, too, screamed for all she was worth. As the doctors held her up for us to look at her, I distinctly remember her becoming suddenly silent as Anna spoke to her.

By this time, the chief surgeon seemed to be strutting even though he was still standing in the same place. The nurses all appeared to be smiling beneath their masks as they danced around the room, taking care of business. I remember the students applauding as little Emma was brought to the recovery room. The mood of the room was one of elation, three big, beautiful, loud, healthy babies delivered in the space of two minutes tend to do that to a room full of medical people. I bent down and kissed Anna and spoke a few quiet words. I have no idea what I said or even if she heard me. The room was buzzing with activity, but it all seemed to be just a quiet blur that neither of us noticed. Anna's eyes seemed to be relaxed for the first time in months. This was a lovely moment for us.

A nurse broke the spell, asking me if I wanted to go next door and meet the babies. I walked into an adjacent room, equal in size to the surgical room. This room had its own doctors and nurses all busy bustling from one task to the next. The nurse said to feel free to move around in this room. As I stood there dumbfounded by all the choices I had, it struck me for the first time that this was much different from the birth of our first child.

I looked at the first crib holding Claire and thought I should go say hi. Then I glanced at the second crib holding a screaming Quinn, and I felt that I should try to settle him down. Then I glanced at the last crib holding Emma, who was just as mad as Quinn, and I thought that I should help her too! I wanted to go in three directions at once. I suspected that this would be a dilemma that would plague me for the foreseeable future.

I wandered around, introducing myself to my latest tax deductions for at least a half hour. Big, bad Quinn seemed huge and healthy at six pounds eleven ounces while Claire was remarkably calm and still. Emma was so incredibly tiny at four pounds seven ounces I was afraid to touch her. She just didn't seem real, more like a little china doll than a real live baby, but the nurses assured me that all the babies were doing great. Once the babies were all checked out, the nurses wrapped them up and brought them over to meet their mother. It turns out that this triplet birth set a record for combined triplet-baby birth weight at the hospital.

As the first baby met Anna, the doctors were still sewing her up. Nevertheless, Anna was more than excited to meet her little boy. They looked at each other for a few minutes while Anna whispered at him. Soon little Emma appeared already asleep, and I watched as Anna studied this little treasure until Claire came out to meet Mom. Claire was remarkably alert and calm and looked right back as Anna talked to her.

Soon the doctors finished with Anna, and the babies were all packed up and ready to travel to the nursery. So, the nurses got Anna packed in and began pushing her back to the recovery room. As they pushed her into the hall, three little carts, each containing a newborn, were waiting for their mom. The caravan progressed down several hallways until it reached the entrance to Anna's room. As we came through the double doors, the procession was greeted by almost a hundred people, all applauding as we passed by.

By now, these nurses, orderlies, and doctors were Anna's friends, having taken care of her during the most challenging time of her life. Many of them were crying; they were so happy for her. They all knew that on many different occasions, it appeared that we might not be lucky enough to make it home with even one healthy baby. They all were a part of, and witness to, the pain and suffering that Anna went through.

Every one of them saw daily how hard Anna fought for those babies, and each person felt more than a little ownership and a whole lot of pride in Anna and in themselves. They all played a role in making possible the three perfectly healthy bundles of joy that were preceding Anna down the hall. Each one of those nurses giggled and squealed in delight as the babies passed by. And each nurse made a point of whispering some sort of congratulation in her ear as Anna paraded past. It must have taken fifteen minutes for Anna and the babies to make their way through this happy crowd. This was a perfect day.

Claire's Special Day

∞∞∞

I'm told to hurry—that something is wrong. I find my wife in a wheelchair holding our baby while a nurse takes Polaroids of them. In a hushed emergency room, technicians hurry to their tasks while carefully avoiding eye contact with us. They know that babies this damaged don't last. Suddenly the curtains jump to the side, and a voice interrupts the sound of sneakers and busy machines.

"She is in trouble." The words spill from behind a mask. "Sign this."

I'm dazed—the voice says something about a blood clot and dying kidneys.

"This gives us permission to get her to another hospital. We can't help her here, but they have a new drug that might."

A nurse waves me into the picture, and a few flashes later, they take the newborn from her mother. They place the baby in a plexiglass vessel brimming with all manner of dials and knobs. We watch as this ark is put onto an ambulance, which quickly moves down the drive. It disappears in a blur of flashing lights, and I look down to see my wife sobbing into the pictures of her girl.

The new hospital brims with confident doctors. Hands thrust reams of forms at me to read and sign. Our baby is quickly hooked to machines, and soon wires and tubes emerge from every available possibility. An incubator keeps her tiny, still, naked body warm and bright, while another machine gives her breath.

Tests, small and large, happen as medical staff rush in and out, consumed in procedures.

From among the confusion, white coats appear, stick out hands, and ask me to follow them. I do until we reach a small, cold room. We sit, and mouths begin to speak.

"She now has bleeding on the brain." The voice echoes.

Because of this, they do not want to give her the medicine that would save her kidneys.

"Why save the kidneys if it'll kill the brain?" a mouth mumbles, turning away.

An awkward pause—all eyes avoid mine—clumsy looks, and nervous fidgets. Then I watch another mouth say, "Your daughter is very, very sick, and there are a lot of things against her right now. Our prognosis is not good. We recommend that you consider letting us turn off—"

A loud knock interrupts. My wife is on the phone.

"They're still doing tests, honey, but she looks good . . ."

I find the chaplain and ask him to baptize our baby. As he performs the ceremony, I stand there holding her tiny hand. While he speaks, I count wires and tubes, watch bubbles rise and fall. Numbers dance on screens, and fluids drip from bags as he gently blesses this tiny soul. The room swirls around this eddy of hope as nurses rush to care for other babies too. He shakes my hand, crosses her again, and gently asks about last rites before he disappears into a watery blur.

She's just two days old. I've never held her or even heard her cry. Are her eyes blue? Two days old. Claire's special, special day!

Daddy's Special Day

∞∞∞

W e visited in shifts
      So that she would never be alone.
      And we learned the role of nurses
In the hopes that we could help.

We moved her limbs and petted her,
And we held her tiny hand.
We cleaned her lips with Q-tips,
And we combed her silky hair.

And we learned
To read the doctor's charts
To watch for answers
To our prayers.

Soon one week turned to two,
Then two weeks turned to three,
But the doctors gave us little hope
And said our dreams would not come true.

So we played her *Mary Poppins*
And sang "Twinkle, Twinkle, Little Star."
And we brought her tapes of nature,
Of wind, and rain, and waves.

We brought photos of her siblings,
And we taped them on her bed.
We told stories about her home
And the happy times to come.

Her grandmothers stopped in to meet her
And made a great big fuss.
Her aunts came by to ooh and aah,
And friends brought cards and gifts.

We even brought big sister in
So she could meet her girl,
And we took lots and lots of photos
To show the crowd at work.

We watched her charts
And prayed out loud,
"Please, God,
Give us hope."

Then one day,
Things got worse,
And the doctor
Brought bad news.

He said, "She's had a setback,
And the machines can help no more."
He righteously assured us
That Claire would soon be gone.

Then calmly, he advised us,
That we should make some plans.
But plans like that we just couldn't do,
We wanted so much more.

Instead, we talked about our dreams
And about the love we had.
We sat there feeling helpless
And didn't know what to do.

So we held her hand
And prayed like mad
For "please, God, one day more."

And one day came
And one day passed

And still, we had our girl.

And then one more
And then some more
And soon days drifted by.

Her chart showed things were changing,
And the doctors didn't know why.
They read the chart,
Then looked at her,

And then read the chart some more.
They scratched their heads
And met in groups,
But they didn't know what to do.

But the nurses seemed to smile a lot
And look us in the eye.
Then one sunny day,
As I sat watching Claire,

A cold wind seemed to pierce the room,
And the white coats did appear.
They stuck out hands,
Said, "Come this way,"

To a small, cold place I did.
I watched them fidget nervously,
And I feared what they would say.

The words they spoke
Seemed strange to them,
And I couldn't believe my ears.

"We don't know why ...
She's doing well ...
Far more than we could hope ...

She's a special girl ...
We'll miss her here,
But now Claire can go home."

They shook my hand
And scratched their heads
And left me all alone.

And as they did,
A voice called out,
"Your wife is on the phone."

"Isn't it great . . ."
"No, I can't wait . . ."
"Yes, she's coming home!"

But then I heard another voice;
It was shaky, but it was clear.
It spoke a phrase

That was new to me,
But those words
I won't forget.

"Would you like to hold your baby now?"

The tubes are gone,
The wires, too,
No more dancing screens.

All machines,
Now put away,
The nurses focus too.

Gone now are the doctors,
And their puzzled looks.
All directed someplace else,
To another needing face.
A simple scene is all that's left;
It's timeless, and it's true.
Just a daddy holding baby
And a bond between the two.

A Little Night Music

∞∞∞

It's 2:00 a.m., and the last of the babies have finally gone back to sleep. Given that I find myself wide awake, I thought to take advantage of all the quiet that currently exists in the house to pen some long overdue thank you notes. Let me say that Anna and I are completely overwhelmed with all the beautiful and thoughtful gifts you have all showered us with. We have yet to buy a diaper! We feel truly blessed. Thank you.

You have probably all heard we almost lost Claire but after a long battle she is home now and doing quite well. In fact, she is perhaps the most interactive of the three, and it looks like she will be the first to roll over. Quinn will clearly be the first to fit into his father's clothes, as he appears to have his father's appetite and is growing accordingly. Emma is the enigma of the group and is somehow able to cry while breathing both out and in. It's really something to hear! All of them have started to smile and make noises other than screaming at us.

After four months as the parent of triplets, I can report that it is an incredible experience. It is a cornucopia of emotions supported by a platform of exhaustion. On the happy end of the scale, it is exhilarating, beautiful, and just flat-out amazing. A regular cute fest! There is nothing like watching these three sweet little cherubs happily snuggled together or discovering each has distinct, fully developed personalities and tendencies. On the not-so-happy end of the scale, it is exhausting, and often humbling, and ultimately demoralizing. It is a nonstop, relentless barrage of responsibility, demands, and duties.

But as I look back on these first four months of life with triplets, the thing that has struck me the most is that there is just a lot more life to live. For example, have you ever said to yourself, "I wish there were more hours in the day"? Well, there are! Eight of them! Most people just sleep during them. With triplets, sleep is, more often than not, unfortunately not an option.

A day for most parents has a beginning, a period of activity, and an end, culminating in a period of rest and recovery. For us, a day cannot be clearly delineated as a single twenty-four-hour period. Instead, it is not so clearly defined, and it often blends together with other days to create one long epic known as infancy. In fact, time itself is no longer measured in simple units of hours, minutes, and days. Instead, time in the triplet world is measured by feedings and changings. Feedings and changings are the only units of measurement that have any meaning to a triplet parent. Minutes, hours, and days are just words used by the outside world to document their day.

A full feeding means feeding all of the babies once and getting them back to sleep. The goal of an adult caught in the trap of triplet feeding cycles is to make it to the end of a period, whether it's the 1:00 a.m., 2:00 a.m., 3:00 a.m., 4:00 a.m., 5:00 a.m., or 6:00 a.m. feeding. The length of the start and end of a feeding cycle can only be guessed. As parents, we have a general idea as to when a feeding cycle will start, but predicting when one will end is unfortunately impossible. There are just too many factors that can alter the progression of the period. Still, it is the goal, because at the end of the cycle exists a mythical, elusive, and fleeting land of peace and tranquility, jealously guarded by a trio of lightly sleeping babies.

The beginning of a feeding cycle is clearly defined by the sudden explosion of ear-piercing, 100-decibel cries. Quinn can be sleeping soundly one minute and be doing a car alarm imitation the next. No warm-up, just instant full volume for no apparent reason. The actual feeding process can be divided into several stages: preparation, feeding, burping, and cleanup. The challenge of preparation—and most things with triplets—is that everything has to be done with one hand. This is because the hungry baby demands the right to supervise food preparation. They comment on its progress in the loudest possible way and thus must be held in at least one arm during the entire process.

The obvious solution would be to leave the screaming dervish in the crib while you prepare the food. It would then seem logical to place the screamer in a neutral site while you make the food. Unfortunately, we soon discovered that no place in the house is soundproof enough to be protected from the lung power of an angry triplet. If you hold them and allow them to supervise while you prepare the food, they actually idle down the howling as long as they perceive proper progress.

Even though the infant cannot talk, it is always obvious what their 3:00 a.m. screams are saying: "Feed me now! I don't want to wait for my food. Why do I have to wait? If I have to wait one second longer, I'll scream so loud that I'll pop your eardrums and wake up the rest of my gang."

Nothing is more frightening to a parent of triplets than the dreaded 3:00 a.m. eruption that is a group screaming session. Walking into a room containing three infants screaming at the top of their lungs is like sticking your head into the back of a jet engine. It is just inconceivable how loud they can be, and the pain lingers for hours. Pound for pound, I am positive that triplets make more noise than a jet!

Parental recovery from one of these episodes can take days. Symptoms displayed by a parent who has suffered through a 3:00 a.m. eruption are ringing in the ears, shaky hands, and profuse sweating. Repeated exposure causes slurred speech and one pupil that seems to be fully dilated all the time. Once a parent has experienced a triplet eruption, nothing will prevent that parent from doing whatever it takes to avoid it, including learning how to do everything with one hand.

So, with a baby in one hand, you try to prepare a bottle. This, of course, is a process clearly meant for those with two hands. The truth is that pretty much everything you do as a parent of triplets, you learn to do with one hand. With practice, it is entirely possible to use a manual can opener, wash dishes, shave, get dressed, fold laundry, and even tie your shoes with just one hand. It is incredible what you can hold in the crook of your neck, your armpit, or between your teeth. It is even possible to carry and bottle feed two babies at once.

The real work starts once the bottle is empty. This marks the beginning of the grueling burping stage. I've heard that this can be as short as just a few minutes, but I've never seen it last less than thirty minutes and have never been able to make it last less than forty minutes myself. More often than not, it continues for the better part of an hour.

Proper burping is essential because it releases trapped air from a baby's tummy. It is imperative to get this air out of the belly because if left there, it can be compressed. When this happens, it is then capable of propelling the contents of the baby's stomach several feet across the room. I'm not kidding, several feet. Most times, it is propelled out onto . . . me! I am convinced that little Emma is actually capable of expelling much more than she took in. It has gotten so routine for Emma to vomit all over my just cleaned shirt that I hardly even break conversation when it happens.

If you take the detour to the cleanup stage, then you must also go back to the start of the process. This is because the baby's newly empty stomach is still hungry, and they start crying all over again. This detour back to bottle preparation, feeding, and burping will subtract at least another hour from what most people call sleep.

Even successful controlled burps are somewhat messy. Most burps result in at least a little spit up happily expelled from the child. Early on, we jealously guarded the clothes of both children and ourselves from these tiny eruptions. After the proper level of exhaustion sets in, I could really care less about these little spots as long as the baby burps and falls asleep. The result is that, by the end of the day, any shirt you are wearing can tell the story of exactly how tired you are and how many times you've burped the babies. The one clear thing is that you never get more than one wear out of a shirt before washing. Dry-cleaned items are never worn in the presence of triplets.

The actual process of burping is itself an exhausting ritual. You obviously hold the baby in the conventional way and pat and rub the baby gently but firmly on the back. The problem is that they never seem to burp—especially Emma. You pat and pat and rub and rub until you can't see straight. Just when you are sure that your hand is about to fall off, the baby starts to cry like a burp is eminent, thus inspiring you to even more and more patting and rubbing. Still, nothing happens, or worse, you get a fake burp that leads you to believe that your job is done.

This is a very frightening event because it can trick you into thinking that the child is content and that projectile vomit has been averted. Typically, the child will get very quiet and still, just like on a real burp. They may even shut their eyes as if to sleep. The ugly reality is that they are getting ready to hurl, and the knowledgeable parent will know this. They will then continue to pat and pat and pat well past this initial fool's gold of burps. I am sure that since the birth of our triplets, I have put on at least an inch of muscle around my wrists from burping babies.

So now you've made it past the burping stage, and you're holding a sleeping infant. Your heart races with the thought of a little REM sleep of your own. You carefully switch the child to a horizontal position to see if sleep remains. Still the child sleeps, and your pulse quickens—dreams are just moments away for you now. You gently lower the child into the crib an inch at a time like you're trying to defuse a bomb. This lowering can take a minute or two to the parent who "understands" the ramifications of the action. The baby's back touches the mattress, and now you stay perfectly still—you don't dare to even breathe. You carefully look for signs of stirring, and seeing none, you slowly pull your hands from beneath the child—so far so good. You stand there, elated, filled with joy at your terrific accomplishment, the sleeping child. You watch for a minute or two just to make sure, then you turn to leave filled with a great sense of accomplishment, ready to sleep as deeply as you possibly can. Suddenly your world explodes. As you move from the crib, incredible screams burst your ears. The child is awake and mad and has fooled you with a fake burp. You must respond quickly now and get back to burping before a full three-headed eruption occurs. This process is usually repeated several times with each baby at each feeding.

Actually, several other possible scenarios could happen at this point. More often than not, you never get the baby into the bed. Instead, they wake up when you turn them horizontal or as you lower them into the crib. It is a source of never-ending curiosity for me that a baby can be asleep in your arms in a horizontal position. Yet, without changing their position, they will wake up as you lower them into the crib. It's as if they have some sort of an altimeter alarming them that you are trying to actually end this process.

Indeed, none of this is news to any parent. A singlet is every bit as capable as a triplet of being profoundly disruptive to the parental lifestyle. When we had our training baby (our first child), I was sure that no parent could have ever suffered such an ungodly loss of sleep and change in lifestyle. In my more blithering moments, I remember thinking how nice it would be just to have a few hours alone with my thoughts or my hobbies or my wife. With triplets, I hope for just a few minutes to use the bathroom. Now I look back at my days as a parent of only one and pshaw the notion that it was a challenge. I hear new parents complain about getting up five or six times a night with their puny singlet litter. How about twenty-three times a night! Singlet sminglet— that ain't nothing!

It isn't just two more babies. It's two more sentient beings, individuals with their own requirements and agendas competing for and demanding attention. Additionally, they seem to operate as a team and appear to have a sixth sense about when a parent is suddenly free and trying to relax. It's singlets cubed! Each is fully able to sleep while one of the others scream and yell and generally occupy the parents' every waking minute. It is the sleeping baby that is the most dangerous to a parent's mental health because a sleeping baby awakes fully rested and ready to go. As a parent, you frantically try to get the awake child fed, changed, and back to sleep before a sleeping child wakes up so that you can grab a few minutes of sleep for yourself. However, rest is always fleeting because two others have been soundly sleeping for hours now. It is a sure thing that one of them will suddenly wake up from the noise of your head hitting the pillow.

The obvious solution would be to wake them up all at once and get one big group feeding out of the way. Triplets wake easily when you don't want them to—from a hiccup from a sibling or the sound of a passing comet. But they are impossible to wake if you actually want them to be awake. I have tried everything from jiggling to a bath, loud noises, and pleading to wake up our triplets for feeding on our schedule. None of these techniques work. Instead, triplets just sleep through all attempts to wake them until about fifteen minutes after you have given up and gone to sleep.

But for all of the lack of sleep and use of our arms, triplets are a very cool thing. It's fascinating to compare and contrast their development. It's incredible to see all those little arms and legs flailing happily about as they gleefully interact with their big sister. In short, I wouldn't recommend having three at once, but I wouldn't trade this experience for anything in the world.

Proud Papa

∞∞∞

I'm the father of triplets—
    Plus one
    I love them all
I am blessed by them
Possessed by them

A mouth screams

I feed them and hold them
I protect and warm them
I treasure and teach them
I am blessed

A mouth screams

I am also a husband
I love her too
I will protect her
Serve her
Honor and obey
I treasure her

A mouth screams

All I do is not enough
A mouth screams
The need is so much
I am overwhelmed
I fail them

My best won't do
They need more

A mouth screams

The mouth needs help
It can't speak
Frantic searches but
It screams
And screams and screams.

I'm lost

A mouth screams
She loves them too
She is at peace
A mouth screams
This is her world
They complete her
A mouth screams

I am alone
I dream of her
Am compelled by her
Controlled by her

A mouth screams

Nights are void of her
They've stolen her smile
Her passion, her life,
From me

A mouth screams
Our oldest is like me too
Our oldest misses her most
Our oldest has needs too

A mouth screams

Conceived of dreams
Our future hope

She is our pride and joy
A mouth screams

Born of dreams
She'll always be first
Except now
She's last

A mouth screams

Now she is fourth
Now she gets less
If any at all
Now when she dreams
It's of yesterdays

A mouth screams

The numbers overwhelm
Mouths scream
The focus is so unclear,
Time disappears
Mouths scream
Good intentions fail

I care so much
A mouth screams
I know that is not enough
I know more is needed

I would slay armies
And build them a fortress
To protect them from harm

A mouth screams

But all I would do
Mouths just don't care
They just want! They just need
Whatever I do
It is never enough
So what do I do

A mouth screams and screams and screams and screams . . .

A Trip to the Mall

∞∞∞

One of the biggest mistakes we made as new triplet parents was in thinking that we should never try to leave the house. What we learned over time is that we were foolish to ever try to stay home. In fact, we learned that the more we are gone, the better. This is not to say that we don't love our house, because we do love it. It is because we love it that we realize the best thing we can do for it is to run away from home.

The simple reality is that if we stay home, the house will get trashed. Not part of it, not a few rooms of it, but the whole house, inside and out. Yes, we discipline our kids, and yes, we teach them to put things back where they got them. However, sooner or later, the phone will ring or we will have to make a meal, change a diaper, or go potty. During that incredibly small amount of time, there is the possibility that the chain reaction will begin. It is very much like lighting the booster rockets on an Apollo moon rocket. Once you start those rockets, they can't be stopped. They just go and go until they are completely burned out.

On a typical weekend morning, our family, like all families, wakes up. At that instant, and until the chain reaction starts, the house is usually perfectly clean. The toys are in the toy boxes, the dishes are done, and the carpets and floors are clean. All this cleaning, of course, all gets done late the night before, after the children have all finally fallen asleep. Every morning, we can find the phone and see through the windows, and the dog still looks like he is black in color. When the kids wake up, the first thing that they want to do is cuddle with Mommy, and the world is good. However, sooner or later, they want to be fed, and usually, this is the start of the ballistic missile ride that is to become our day.

You see, the kids are OK and the house is under control as long as they are being supervised every single second. It's when you shut your eyes during a sneeze that all hell breaks loose. It's when one of them acts up and needs a time-out or when the salesman calls. I've timed it—little Emma can run downstairs, open the toy box, and pull out her collection of miniature farmyard animals in just eighteen seconds. I've timed it, and it takes baby Claire twenty-one seconds to go from the bedroom to the top of the bathroom sink counter to begin painting on the mirror with toothpaste. It only takes little buddy Quinn thirty-four seconds to run outside to the sandbox. Once there, he collects a bucket of sand and returns to the living room floor to play with his toy trucks in that sand. Any one of these whimsical activities can be the match that lights the fuse that launches chaos.

Think about it: How long does it take you to go potty in the morning? Go ahead, try it yourself. I've timed it with a stopwatch, and I can't go faster than thirty-two seconds when I go potty first thing in the morning—or any other time of the day for that matter. And it's not that the other parent is doing nothing while this bathroom race is taking place. No, that parent is busy trying to make sure that they don't have to put the toothpaste back in the tube, or that the miniature farmyard animals don't stampede into the pool. And even if that parent is a success as a dentist and as a cowboy, there is still the matter of the heavy machinery moving sand around the living room.

The sand itself in the living room isn't really that big a deal—it's the fact that it takes at least four or five minutes to clean up that sand. If Pandora's box can be opened in just thirty-two seconds, imagine how much toothpaste can be squeezed and smeared by baby Picasso in four or five minutes. By the way, in case you are wondering, it takes much longer to clean up tooth-paste than it does to clean up sand.

The point of this is that if you suddenly wake up one morn-ing and discover that you have triplets, the first thing you want to do is to pack up the children and leave the house for the day. You can wait to pee. You can go potty at a gas station. Let the gas sta-tion people clean up the sand.

When you leave the house for the day, it really doesn't mat-ter where you go. Triplets love to go anywhere. They just love to be out and about, but zoos and parks are probably their favorites. Any place will do as long as it's not home. For parents, some places are definitely more fun than others. For example, if you have a friend that you lost a bet with, say on a football game, make sure that you and the family visit his house personally to pay off that bet. While you're at his home, make sure that you use the bath-room a time or two. As soon as the sand is spilled in the living room, act like you're upset with the kids and make a point of loudly saying, "We can't take you kids anywhere." Then quickly leave.

I've also thought that it would be fun someday to show up at the house of an apparently wealthy person who happens to be a complete stranger. We would then get the kids out of the car and walk up to the big front door en masse with all our bags and suit-cases and ring the doorbell.

When the owners answer the door, we would announce that we finally made it. I would then go on about how long the drive was and how cranky the kids are and just generally burst in like we are a long lost family and are expected. All of this before they can get a word in edgewise.

When we finally do give them a chance to speak and they ask who we are, we would then turn to them with great indig-nation and say, "Aren't you my mom's sister's great-aunt Millie?" When they inform us that no, they are not Aunt Millie, we will act horrified, as if the directions that we got from the sister were all wrong. By this point, of course, the house would be a total mess, so we would quickly gather up the kids, tip the homeowner a few dollars, and promptly leave.

The reason for doing this would simply be to see the expression on this person's face. Imagine it as they stand there on the stoop, dollar bills flapping in the breeze, wondering what the hell just happened to them as they stand in a pile of sand at their feet. Luckily for my family, and apparently wealthy homeowners everywhere, I am not a good enough actor or brave enough to even consider doing such a thing.

A saner outing for the family is going to a museum, zoo, or mall. From the strictly male point of view, going to the mall with infant triplets is one of the greatest things a guy can do. Moms like to shop, and that leaves Dad all alone to watch the babies.

Poor Dad, you say? Dads, if you have never stood all alone in the middle of a mall with a triplet stroller full of babies, then you really need to find a way to make it happen. Women love babies, and malls are full of women. I am not an attractive guy. Maybe I'm OK looking on a good day if my hair isn't doing weird things, but for the most part, women have never gone out of their way to talk to me. Ah, but when you're the proud Daddy of three adorable little cherubs, then you, sir, are a great big beautiful rock star.

Women don't just look into the stroller and smile at the baby like they do with a cute singlet. With infant triplets, it turns into a feeding frenzy. Women gather around, jump up and down, paw at you, and generally get so close to you, that you can see their fillings when they smile. Old women, young women, all women!

Infant triplets are like the color red to a bull or blood to a shark. Women just can't help themselves. We're talking about The Beatles on *The Ed Sullivan Show* kind of reactions here. The best part is you don't have to do or say anything other than "yes they are triplets." And "yes, they are mine." After that, just stand there, smile, and watch the "reeelly big shoooo."

Infant triplets are catnip to women. Let's say a bachelor needed a wife in thirty minutes or less. I have total confidence that if that man carried my infant triplets into a beauty parlor, he could walk out with a new wife ten minutes later. An unscrupulous man could make a fortune renting his infant triplets out to young men looking to get lucky with the opposite sex.

The other fun thing about going to malls with triplets is that it really makes you aware of—how do I say this nicely—how stupid people are.[2] The first time we went out in public with the babies, we went to the mall. Anna was wearing her "I'm the Proud Mother of Triplets" T-shirt, and I was wearing my "I'm the Proud Father of Triplets" T-shirt. My wife was pushing our triplet stroller, and all of the babies were dressed identically.

I noticed a normal looking, middle-aged, apparently healthy woman looking at us from across the concourse. She made her way over and looked into the stroller like she stumbled upon a pile of gold. Then she studied my wife and me. Her study included clearly looking at the bold lettering on our T-shirts. She then turned to my wife, pointed and the babies, and with great sincerity, slowly, like we were hard of hearing asked, "ARE. THOSE. BABIES. TRIPLETS?"

Stunned at the question, we nodded politely and said yes. She shook her head as if we had slapped her hard. She then gathered her composure and asked, "WERE. THEY. BORN. AT. THE. SAME. TIME?"

Anna and I glanced at each other, and then we again nodded politely and said yes.

The woman again shook her head. Clearly in a stupor now, she recovered and posed the question, "ARE. THEY. RELATED?"

We nodded yes. She stood there in bewildered silence, looking at Anna's tummy. She then leaned forward, put her hand to the back of her head, looked down at each one of the babies, looked at Anna, and asked, "ARE. YOU. THEIR. MOTHER?"

She studied Anna's face and looked around at all of us as if she woke up from a prizefight gone wrong and didn't know where she was. We politely drifted away, feeling like we had just had a conversation with the Cheshire cat.

After that, we have never worn our "I'm the Proud Mother/Father of Triplets" T-shirts again. However, it has really made no difference. If we set out to have a contest that required the winner to ask the most stupid question, this woman would not have won. Sadly, she was rather typical. Some of the really "winning" questions we've been asked make me wonder how these people remember to breathe every day. We've had people ask, "Did we know they were triplets when they were born?"

My wife has been asked, "Were you there when they were born?" and "Were you pregnant when this happened?"

I'm not kidding about or exaggerating these statements. There is something about seeing infant triplets that just makes some folks lose all blood flow to their brains. Other examples include:

"Were you planning on having triplets?"

"Are they all twins?

"Are you sure?"

"Why is one a boy?"

Pointing to our fourth child, a person asked, "She's not a triplet, too, is she?"

"Did you get a lot of money and prizes?"

"Do they ever cry at the same time?"

"Do you have to feed them all?"

"Do they share diapers?"

"Do they have the same father?"

"Why is that one bigger?"

"Do they sing?"

"Are they real?"

"Are they natural or fake?"

And my personal favorite: "How did this happen?"

Actually, that is a great question. I'm still trying to figure that out myself.

Couches, Leaf Rakes, and Tin Cans

∞∞∞

If I got to make the rules, the eleventh commandment would state that all toys have to meet a minimum size requirement. This minimum size has nothing to do with child safety—such as whether or not a child can swallow it—although, for obvious reasons, that is also important. Instead, the size requirement of toys should be determined by two criteria. The first criterion is that it must be easy for adults to keep track of and clean up. The second criterion is that a plaything should not be able to inflict mental or physical pain on a parent. You see, while protecting the baby is obviously the most critical thing, protecting the sanity of the parent is an aspect of toy design that has long been overlooked.

So then, beside child safety, what are the standards that should be applied to the design and manufacture of children's toys? How big is too big? How small is too small? There needs to be a universal standard, or tool, that can be readily available and explicitly tailored to the needs of each individual family. I submit that there is such a tool, and it currently exists in most American homes. I feel that perhaps the best device to gauge toy size is the typical American family couch.

As you know, couches eat things. Think about how many buckets full of change, keys, and television remotes you've found in the cushions of your couch during your lifetime. Well, in addition to these mundane items, sofas can also consume large quantities of toys. This ability to eat makes the couch the perfect tool for judging which toys a family may own.

Of course, the quality and age of the couch can have a significant impact on its ability to measure and/or eat toys. They would, therefore, determine what kind of toys that family can have. A high-quality couch with tight cushions is the worst for parents because it is so well constructed that it eats almost no toys at all. This means that the kids can have even the smallest of toys.

However, if your couch is beaten up, old, and cheap, it will eat all toys, which means that the kids don't get any toys at all. Our couch is so beat up and loose around the cushions that pretty much any size toy will fall between the cushions. The other day I found a rocking horse stuck between the cushions. Our couch can even eat the kids, which they think is great fun.

Were the eleventh commandment to be passed into law, it would dictate that our kids get pretty much no toys. The point here is that if there are no toys, then you do not have to clean them up. Lately, all we do is clean up toys. Of course, if you happen to get a new couch, then you would have to get an entirely new set of toys because all the old ones would no longer conform to the eleventh commandment.

The one positive aspect of the fact that couches eat toys is that this process assures that all toys get played with. As playthings get played with, they inevitably get eaten by the couch and taken out of circulation for a while. The kids then naturally find another toy, and the process is repeated. Once a week or so, after this process has repeated itself about a million times or when our toy box is almost empty, I turn over the couch, pull off the cushions, and dump a cornucopia of plastic bits and pieces. The triplets love this ritual and immediately swarm with glee over the multicolored bounty of joy, like vultures picking a carcass clean. Then the process starts again.

The other reason toys should not be too small is that it makes them very difficult to clean up. Once the triplets have picked over the couch, the toys inevitably cover the living room carpet. Every square inch of it! Thousands of tiny parts! Picking them up one at a time will take forever and lead to degeneration of the spine in the parent doing the picking.

The only efficient way to clean up all these toys is to either replace the carpet or use a leaf rake. A large plastic leaf rake is one of my most valuable domestic tools, because with it, it is possible to clean the carpet of toys in just a few minutes. And if you rake all the toys onto a baby blanket, you can pick up the entire pile and dump it in the toy box in one fell swoop! If you don't like the blanket technique, then use a snow shovel. It is not as elegant a solution, but it is quick, and it is a whole lot easier than stooping to conquer each individual toy. Of course, this is only possible if the toys are not so small that they slip between the fingers of the rake in the first place. Marbles are the worst, and they simply cannot be raked.

This brings us to the second criterion for determining toy size. That is that all toys must be pedagogically friendly. "Pedagogically friendly" defines how small, sharp, and/or hard a toy is. Specifically, it clarifies the pain that a toy is capable of inflicting upon you if you happen to be barefoot and blindly step on it in the middle of the night. If you do step on a toy and it causes you enough pain to cry out, then that toy is not "pedagogically friendly."

Actually, "pedagogically friendly" is an excellent way of describing how severe the explosion of four-letter words stepping on toys provokes. At the top end of the scale is severe toy pain caused by stepping on it. In response, you kick something else and don't even notice it because, compared to the original, the new injuries are just a pleasant distraction. When you step on an "unfriendly" toy, the other grown-ups in the house know it because of the seven or eight "bad" words that spill from your lips. Any toy that is capable of causing this kind of pain is either too small, sharp, or hard and should be recalled and destroyed.

Furthermore, the makers of that toy should be forced to walk around blindfolded and barefoot in a room littered with their product. Jacks and Monopoly game hotels and houses are the absolute worst. Sure, walking on a bed of hot coals is a difficult thing to do, but try stepping on a single jack barefoot. Jacks were initially invented as a medieval torture device, and Monopoly houses are just a modern evolution of that torture.

The reality is that adults in triplet households don't really walk around at night in the dark. It's too dangerous. There are simply too many obstacles to bump into or step on, no matter how good a housekeeper you are. When they must move about at night, parents of triplets do something called the Frankenstein Shuffle.

First, holding your hands out in front about waist high, perform an awkward shuffle. While in this position, move your hands quickly back and forth like a big ugly insect, its antennae jerking around as it searches for the unknown. While your hands flail aimlessly, the actual forward movement is achieved without your feet ever actually leaving the floor. Instead, slowly slide your feet along, toes curled upward, carefully sensing for the inevitable thump! Your feet must never leave the ground because this prevents you from actually stepping on objects small, sharp, and hard.

While it would seem logical to just turn on the lights, this is the last thing a triplet parent will do. Triplets have a sixth sense that other babies do not have that allows them to sense light with their eyes shut and through walls. I think that these extra sensors are located in their skin, or they can actually hear electricity suddenly moving through the wires in the wall.

Anyway, as soon as they sense light, they wake up and want to play or, worse, they wake up mad because you're up to without them. Either way, your sleep for that night is done. Rather than take a chance on that, the triplet parent learns to shuffle and, in fact, do everything else in the dark. By this point in my life, I've already gone to the bathroom several million times, so I can do that blindfolded. I've also made several billion baby bottles, so I don't need my eyes to do that either. What other possible reasons could there be to get up at night?

The other thing I would do if I were writing new commandments would be to write one making it illegal for toys to have more than one part. Toys with more than one part simply do not interest the child, and they just annoy the parents. The triplets may play with all parts of a toy, but they will never use the pieces together the way the manufacturer intended. In fact, the more elements a toy has, the less chance it has of ever being played with. It is an inverse relationship, and it is actually one of the governing laws of the universe. The law of infant interaction states:

A child's interest in a toy is directly correlated to how difficult that toy is to clean up or put together. A child is only interested in a toy with lots of parts long enough to get out of the box and spread it around, and then they will play with the box the toy came in.

The multipart toy law also correlates to getting and receiving baby gifts. If the giver really cares for the parents, then the present will always be something sweet and soft like a baby blanket or pajamas. If the gift giver does not care for the parents, the gift will be a toy in several parts. If the gift giver hates the parents but is compelled for some evil reason to still give a gift, then that gift will always be a toy with several hundred small sharp parts.

Besides, it is my experience that triplets far and away prefer to play with things that are not toys at all. The television remote, for example, is a source of endless fascination for them. They have no idea what it is or does, but all those buttons are triplet catnip. I have witnessed savage fights between triplets when one of them has the remote and another one wants it. Of course, as soon as these fights result in the remote-control top getting ripped off, the batteries spill out. This one-part toy is suddenly six parts, and they are no longer remotely interested in it.

In addition to remotes, pots and pans are also of great interest to the triplets. They are shiny, loud, and only one part. Our triplets play with our pots, pans, and lids almost every day. I've witnessed pan lids used correctly make great Frisbees and cymbals, and to shield against the attacks of remote-stealing or biting babies! If you throw a top just right, you can almost hit the birdcage. Pots make perfect hats. Pans make great sleds, and all of these items are apparently a lot of fun to throw down a flight of stairs.

But even more cherished than cookware and television remote controls is the one "toy" that the triplets play with every day above all other toys. Canned goods! Yes, canned goods! You can use canned goods as blocks, balls, musical instruments, chew toys, and of course, weapons. Cans can be dropped, rolled, bowled, piled, and generally scattered to all parts of the house. Cans consist of only one part, and they are cheap, durable, and shiny. Also, they work great as hammers for when you need to adjust a potted plant, and they make neat marks when you beat them on the VCR.

Cans are also fun to throw. When you throw them at the dog, he moves very fast, and that is a lot of fun to watch if you are a two-year-old triplet. Cans can be thrown down the stairs, in the pool, and off the balcony. Best of all, cans make a really distinct and apparently funny noise when you throw them in front of Daddy's lawn mower. Daddy makes weird noises then too. Cans also have great paper labels that can be removed, shredded, and chewed.

After you eat the labels, you can stick the gooey wads to windows, doors, the dog, and each other. Our pantry is very well stocked with a wide variety of foods. However, since none of the cans in our pantry have labels, finding the particular food that you want is a bizarre form of lottery. Last year, instead of cranberry sauce with our Thanksgiving turkey , we had sauerkraut. It was good!

Baby Clothes

∞∞∞

One of the most challenging things about having triplets is keeping track of baby clothes and keeping them all separated for the appropriately sized child. If the triplets happened to be similarly sized and of the same sex, this might not be such a problem. They could each just wear whatever came out of the laundry basket first. But our triplets are all different sizes. The boy is huge, and each girl is a distinct size smaller, so they all have to wear their own clothes. But even though the babies are different sizes, their clothes all look the same size when you're trying to sort them. At least to dads.

By contrast, mothers can sort baby clothes without even looking at them. They have a sixth sense about all things baby. They can just touch an outfit or smell it, and they intuitively know which child it fits. I am not blessed with such powers. I have to hold each piece up to the child to see if it fits. If it doesn't fit, I have to find the next child and repeat the process until I find the child that the outfit matches. While the babies think this game of hide-and-seek is fun, it turns folding and sorting a basket of clothes into an all-night project.

Yes, baby clothes come with labels, but again fathers cannot read them. They are written in mother-ese. The code, written for and by mothers, requires the proper chromosome to decipher it. Men can read the letters on these labels, but no matter how hard we try, we are not genetically equipped to infer their meaning.

For example, a tag might read T12-18. This means that the garment is supposed to fit a child between twelve and eighteen months. This makes no sense, as twelve to eighteen months is not a size; it's time. Clothing can't be measured by time—it has to be measured by size, inches, feet, or yards, and all things metric are sizes.[3] The adult equivalent would be going to a garment store and buying size 40 pants because you're forty years old. It's stupid, it does not work, and it makes me angry because I just cannot seem to get it. So, for sorting purposes, the tags on baby clothes are useless to me.

In desperation, I invented a tool to help solve this problem. I put each child on a piece of cardboard and then carefully and quickly traced the outline of his or her little body in crayon. I then cut out this shape and kept it in the laundry room so that sorting is simply a matter of checking clothes to each cutout.

This worked great until our four-year-old found these little figures and decided to adopt and name them. She then decided that she needed to make a few hundred more of her own to play with. The cutouts that I made have long since been absorbed into her inventory of silhouettes. This makes finding and using them for their intended purpose even more frustrating than playing hide-and-seek with the babies.

The other problem with infant clothes is that they are tiny. A full load of my laundry consists of three or four pairs of jeans and maybe seven or eight shirts. This takes about two minutes to fold and or hang up. A full load of baby clothes is at least two hundred small items. Even if they were all for one child, this takes about thirty minutes per basket to fold. This is much more than can be folded during the halftime of any game or during any six commercials!

And baby socks are impossible. Each sock is the size of an uninflated balloon. And unlike adult socks, infant socks multiply when you put them in the wash. You may put in ten infant socks to get washed, but when they come out, there will always be at least twice that. Of course, like their adult counterparts, these new socks do not match any other socks in your inventory. I guess the good thing is that, because they tend to multiply, you never actually have to buy baby socks.

Infant socks are curious for several other reasons as well. For starters, they are charged with a specific kind of static electricity that makes them stick only to men's dress pants. This static electricity is so strong that the pants and socks need never actually come in contact with each other for the attraction to occur. You can simply walk by a laundry basket, and the sock flies out of the basket and sticks to your pants without you knowing it.

There is nothing worse than standing up to lecture in front of a class full of bright college students and discovering a tiny sock stuck to the zipper zone of your pants. Any chance that you might have had for the students to take you seriously that day is gone the minute that your students notice it and you don't.

Baby Shoes

∞∞∞

Baby shoes are a source of endless curiosity for me. First of all, they cost as much as full-grown adult shoes, even though they are so small they can be made with leftover leather. Apparently, an infant must wear proper shoes for foot support. Since they can't walk or walk very poorly, I don't understand why excellent foot support is essential. Still, my wife assures me that it is necessary.

And why is it that baby shoes are so hard to put on yet they come off so quickly? I'll struggle for five minutes to get a single shoe on. Even if the shoe is certified to fit perfectly, it seems that no amount of wiggling and twisting will get the bleeping shoe on the damned foot.

I think that baby shoes can actually sense that you're going to have a stroke. Every time I am confident that I am about to blackout from the frustration of putting on a baby shoe, it inexplicably slides on foot.

The truly maddening part is that for all of the effort it takes to get the damned shoe installed on the baby's foot, it slides right back off like buttered eggs on Teflon as soon as the child tries to walk. The number of times I've gotten a shoe on one foot only to discover the baby has already managed to knock the one off the other foot is blithering to me. This can go on all day, especially if you are in a hurry because it is, of course, tied to how big a hurry you're in. If you absolutely must leave the house in the next two minutes, then it will take forty minutes to get all of the babies' shoes on.

This assumes, of course, that you can find all of the baby shoes that you need for all of the babies' little feet. You will always be able to find a lot of baby shoes scattered around the house. The problem is finding shoes that fit all of the different size babies that we have. Again, if our kids were the same size, this would be no big deal since the first shoe you found could go on the first foot you managed to catch up to. Heck, most of the time, I wouldn't even care if it was a boy or girl—just put the shoe on any foot, and let's get going. But the shoe must fit, or it's no good. Too small and you can't get it on at all, too big and it falls off even quicker than they usually do. You cannot cheat with baby shoes—they must fit and, no, duct tape is not an option. I've tried it, and it gets all gooey and ruins the shoes.

Baby shoes hide, and I am pretty sure that they communicate and work together to stay hidden. It's like a game of hide-and-seek: you against all of the shoes. As I said, most times, I can easily find twenty shoes in just a few minutes. But these shoes are only spies who give themselves up so that they can feed reports to the hidden shoes that you really need. Usually, you can readily find about eight matching pairs for one size baby, three mismatched pairs for another baby, and four right-footed shoes for the other.

At least the mismatched pairs can be used if you are truly desperate. I've found baby shoes in produce in the vegetable drawer in the refrigerator. They've turned up behind a box of cereal in a cabinet five feet off the floor. I've found a baby shoe in a box of clothing that was sealed and stored before they were even conceived.

The genuinely disturbing thing is that after you return from whatever trip you were late getting to, you can always expect to find several of the shoes that you couldn't see before you left, right out in plain sight, taunting you. "Ollie ollie oxen free."

How can this be? This can't happen unless extraordinary forces are at work here. I maintain that baby shoes are like little superheroes that are alive and that they can actually fly and morph through walls when you aren't looking. How else can you explain a baby shoe in a sealed box?

Baby Teeth

∞∞∞

The triplets bite! Actually, Quinn doesn't bite, but instead, he gets bit. Quinn still hasn't caught on, and he doesn't even see it coming until the girl's teeth release their grip from his back, shoulder, or arm. It just does not occur to him that someone would purposely inflict that kind of pain on him. It is the girls, Emma and Claire, who bite, and they are vicious about it.

Emma is by far the worst as she has evolved into something of a pit bull when it comes to biting. She bites, clamps down, pulls, and twists. It really hurts! When the biting episodes started happening, it was kind of funny and pretty harmless in that none of them had any teeth. Typically, a conflict would break out over a toy or bottle. Before you knew it, the two girls were squaring off, gums flashing in anger at each other like characters in a silly Godzilla movie. Initially, it was kind of like watching mini gladiator wrestling. You know it's wrong and that you shouldn't watch it. Still, it's so unbelievable that you sit there laughing as you watch these mini gladiators try to gum each other into submission. Emma got teeth first, so these gladiatorial episodes quickly became very unfair, and we obviously try to stop them before they get started.

Claire only seldom tries to bite now, but Emma has kept right at it despite any kind of punishment we use to discourage this behavior. Unfortunately for Quinn, it is he who is most often the target of Emmy's anger. Quinn is bigger than the others, and he is somewhat of a tank when it comes to trying to get to what he wants. He may be sitting there perfectly content with his own bottle, but when one of the girls walks by with their bottle, Quinn, for some reason, forgets that he already has one and tries to take the second bottle. This obviously angers the girls, and they bite him.

One day, Quinn got bitten five times. During one painful stretch, he managed to get bitten twice, by two different sets of teeth in the space of two minutes! First, Quinn stole a toy, which got him bit the first time. He was so upset by this that he blindly turned and collapsed in tears right on top of his other sister, who promptly bit him on the other arm in response. At this point, he was rightfully hysterical.

By now, he is so used to being bitten he is starting to not even respond when these bites happened. The last time Claire bit him, leaving her distinct four-tooth tattoo on his forearm, and he hardly looked up from his toy.

Baby Bottles

∞∞∞

Bottles are an incredibly important part of the inventory of the triplet household. We have more bottles than we do toys, and we have a lot of toys. We can't find most of these bottles, but still, we have them somewhere. Consider the number of containers required on a typical day, and you will understand why we own so many.

To start with, we give our triplets two bottles a day filled with just baby formula, because it assures that they get enough of the nutrition they need even if they don't eat well. That makes six bottles. At each of the three formal meals, each baby will have a bottle containing either juice, water, or milk to wash it down. Three meals times three bottles at each meal equals nine more bottles for a running total of fifteen bottles so far. Additionally, the babies usually have an afternoon and a bedtime snack consisting of a treat and a bottle of juice. Then we use three bottles times two snacks or six more bottles for a running total of twenty-one bottles.

Random bottle usage is the next group of bottles we have to factor in. Now we get to the category where the real bottle usage happens. Like everybody else, babies get thirsty throughout the day. Each baby will typically have four additional bottles of water at various times during the day. That's four bottles times three babies for a total of twelve more bottles for a running total of thirty-two bottles.

On top of that, babies like to have a bottle as a sort of

comfort tool. It helps during times of stress, such as when they get hurt, frustrated, scared, or bitten, for example. Since comfort bottles are impossible to predict, I'll just assure you that it is never fewer than ten (10) bottles. Added that to our running total giving us a grand total of forty-two (42) bottles on a typical day. Now the babies don't drink the entire contents of each bottle every time that we give them one. In fact, in the case of comfort bottles, they drink very little. However, even if they only drink a few sips, it is another bottle that has to be prepared and then carefully sterilized or washed.

Preparing or washing a bottle assumes that you can find bottles. Very seldom will any of the triplets sit still and drink. Most of the time, they continue doing whatever interests them while they drink. This includes wandering all over the house with their bottle. The result is that parents must endure the adult equivalent of an Easter egg hunt several times a day. Finding the forty-two bottles that necessity dictates we need every day is not easy. We find bottles under cushions of the couch and beneath the furniture. They end up in every drawer, cabinet, and cupboard of our house. I've located bottles in the toy box, in the barn, and at the bottom of the pool. They've turned up in both cars, the sandbox, and of course, the toilet. The toilet ones I throw out. Last week I found one in the rain gutter. I still can't figure out how it got there.

Early on, I got sick of searching for bottles and decided to just buy enough so that I wouldn't need to go exploring every single time I needed a bottle. That didn't help. We now own somewhere between sixty (60) and one hundred (100) bottles. Having said that, we can only find twenty (20) of them at any given moment, and of those twenty (20) bottles, eighteen (18) seem to always be dirty. This means that every single time you want to make a round of containers for the babies, you have to do the dishes because having two bottles is like having zero bottles.

Whenever you do anything, especially making bottles, it must be done in threes. Making two bottles will just get you scolded by the triplet that doesn't get one and gets the other babies bitten by him. Actually, it is a good thing that we can never find all of the bottles that we own at any one time. Can you imagine trying to find a space to store one hundred (100) bottles? I've figured out that it would take up more square footage than the space occupied by all of our dishes and pots and pans combined.

Learning to Talk

∞∞∞∞

You have to understand that the frustration level for the triplet parent is very high. Actually, I think it's higher for fathers than it is for mothers, or maybe that is just some sort of genetic excuse that this particular father likes to use. Anyway, I know that doesn't forgive my actions, but the ugly reality is that two-year-old triplets are a lot of work and sometimes a lot of frustration. Yes, they are an endless joy, but let us just say that sometimes even the joy part of it gets to be—well, I get overjoyed. Maybe you could handle it better or would direct your frustrations more appropriately, but on occasion, on occasion . . . I swear.

Yes, I know that is totally inappropriate, especially in front of the kids. Still, sometimes I get so overwhelmed by all the joy that the words just spill out. It's not like I'm a shipboard sailor or anything like that. I don't yell or scream or anything awful. On occasion, though, I have been known to mumble, very quietly, an inappropriate word—or two!

I'm sure that most adults swear on occasion. Sometimes some of them even do it in front of the children. However, I am the father of two-year-old triplets that happen to be learning to talk. The triplets are actually doing quite well with talking. They can say all of the common words—*mommy*, *daddy*, *bottle*, and *no*. Most of these words they say pretty clearly, and as parents, we have no problem understanding those words and many other words that they say.

Strangers, however, sometimes have questions following the triplets because, as two-year-old people, they are still working on proper enunciation. However, there are several other words that they have learned, unfortunately, to speak with the clarity of a seasoned Shakespearean actor.

It's not like they hear these words all the time. In most cases, they've only heard these words when I've mumbled them under my breath, and then only from a great distance. All right, I guess sometimes they listen to them from the back seat of the car when I'm driving. Whatever. Triplets are special children, and unlike other children, they seem to have the innate ability to learn instantly the words that they should not know. Having this ability, they quickly incorporate these words into pretty much all of their activities.

Just the other day, I heard little Claire at bedtime express her distaste for brushing her teeth, "Daddy, I don't want to brush my *!*&+% teeth." And Quinn followed with, "and "*!*&+%, I don't want to go to bed, Daddy!" And Emma then pointed out that I "was a "*!*&+% meanie!" However, unlike the sentences I type here, when they use these inappropriate words, it is the bad words that are crystal clear and the rest of the "terms" that are a little mumbled.

My wife recently made it abundantly clear to me that the triplets advanced use of the English language was starting to be noticed by people outside of the house. Actually, she wasn't quite that polite about it. In fact, when she pointed it out to me, she used some inappropriate words of her own, but that is another story.

The point is, she was trying to make it known to me that some of the daycare ladies were a little concerned about how Claire liked to address the other children in the morning. And apparently, Quinn yelled a little too loudly and a little too clearly when he fell off the slide the other day. In my defense, I pointed out to my wife that I have never, ever used the word that Quinn did before. She didn't seem particularly pacified by my restraint with that particular word. The point of this little story is: Why is it that it took the triplets almost two full years to learn to say the word *daddy*, but they can learn instantly the words Daddy has said only one occasion?

A Balance of Power

∞∞∞

Having a balance of power has proved throughout the history of mankind to be a perfect thing. If not for the Allied forces, who's to say what additional horrors the Nazis might have perpetrated. If not the power of the United States, who's to say what the evil Russian Empire might have committed. A balance of power is an important thing, and it is, believe it or not, an essential aspect of the parent-triplet relationship.

While military power can be offset with a direct application of equal or higher military power, balancing the energy in the parent-triplet relationship hangs from a much finer thread. You see, you have to remember that the collective power of triplets is an overwhelming thing. Sure, individually, they are each just a cute, cuddly baby. Still, collectively they are a force capable of creating profound havoc. Think locusts.

Locusts appear on the horizon a tremendous black cloud. They descend down upon that land, leaving waste and desolation on all they encounter. "They are just big grasshoppers for God's sake," you might say. Yes, but there are an awful lot of them. Well, each triplet is equal to about an acre of locusts when it comes to the devastation they can do to a clean house.

So, what do locusts and Nazis have to do with the balance of power and triplets? Well, without some sort of secret weapon to offset triplets' potential for creating havoc, a parent would be defenseless against this cute little horde. In no time at all, all that would be left of the furniture and indeed of the whole house would be a massive pile of toys and crushed crayons. Everything else—walls, roof, floors—would be ripped up and shredded and chewed back into its component atomic elements. So, what is the secret weapon capable of providing that balance of power, you ask? Well, it's shaped like a rocket, and it is liquid fueled. That's right, a baby bottle.

You see, we realized over time that for a triplet parent, bottle time represents opportunity, potential, and protection. It is the chance to clean, cook, or generally get all nature of things done around the house. When adequately distributed, a round of bottles offers the potential to simply relax and try to figure out how to counteract the chaos that is triplets. Finally, a bottle represents protection for the trampling masses that are triplets when they each want to cuddle with Mommy.

A triplet parent with three freshly filled bottles is a parent that is about to get some time to themselves. It might be only ten minutes, but in the world of tiny people, ten minutes represents a lot of freedom. If you hustle, in ten minutes, it is entirely possible to clean several rooms of the house. If you move quickly, ten minutes is enough time to cook a healthy meal for the family, and ten minutes is more than enough time to fold a load of laundry.

Actually, ten minutes is not much time, but as far as laundry goes, ten minutes is enough time to sort through piles of laundry. By sorting through it, you might be able to find clothes that aren't "too" dirty and that you just might be ready to wear one more time.

All right! Ten minutes is not enough time to do much cleaning either. Still, it might be enough time to create a walking path through the toys. Maybe in that time, you could discard baby clothes and shredded newspapers. That way, you don't have to hop from lily pad to lily pad of open carpet to get from point A to point B anymore.

Cooking. All right ten minutes is only enough time to open a couple of cans of food and warm them up. Still, your family is dressed, fed, and . . . well they're dressed and fed, and on many days, that's pretty good.

But bottles mostly represent a balance of power because no matter what priceless keepsake of yours the triplets are about to break, or how high they've managed to climb up into the kitchen cupboards, or even how many of your socks they still have left to flush down the toilet, when they see you start to make bottles, they stop. They stop whatever they are doing and politely gather up behind you and calmly wait for the liquid gold you prepare for them. It is for these few minutes while you make this cherished snack that you have the power in the parent triplet relationship. For the other twenty-three and five-sixths hours of the day—they own you!

A Day

∞∞∞

8:00 p.m.: Put the babies in bed.
8:05 p.m.: Do dishes, clean house, vacuum, do laundry.

9:00 p.m.: Anna reads Kelsey a story.

9:10 p.m.: I try to do some homework.

10:25 p.m.: Kelsey finally falls asleep.

11:30 p.m.: Relax, watch a little TV.

Midnight: I go to bed.

12:08 a.m.: Claire wakes up and wants to be held. Give her a bottle and rock her.

12:25 a.m.: Claire is asleep. I put her back in her crib. She instantly cries and wants out.

12:28 a.m.: I take Claire downstairs. We sit in front of the TV until she falls asleep.

12:40 a.m.: Quinn wakes up, screaming. Anna sits with him in front of the TV until he sleeps.

12:45 a.m.: Emma wakes up, screaming. All babies are now awake and screaming.

1:15 a.m.: We put them in their cribs to cry themselves to sleep.

1:45 a.m.: Quinn is still screaming.

1:48 a.m.: I go out in the yard to bang my head against the apple tree.

1:49 a.m.: I watch a cloud pass in front of the moon. It's pretty.

1:51 a.m.: Take two aspirins for a headache.

1:51 a.m.: I get Quinn out of bed so he won't wake the others.

2:15 a.m.: Quinn falls asleep.

2:17 a.m.: Get in bed. Check that the alarm is set for 7:00 a.m.

2:30 a.m.: Quinn screams, nothing is apparently wrong.

2:32 a.m.: Change diaper, hug for a few minutes.

2:35 a.m.: Give a water bottle and put him back in bed.

2:40 a.m.: Stroke his back until he falls asleep.

2:45 a.m.: Drink a beer.

2:50 a.m.: Lay back down.

3:10 a.m.: Claire wakes up, screaming.

3:11 a.m.: I give her a bottle and take her into our bed.

3:20 a.m.: Wake realizing that the bottle has leaked. Claire's pajamas and the bedsheets are completely soaked.

3:22 a.m.: Change sheets, make a new bottle.

3:29 a.m.: Anna takes two aspirin.

3:35 a.m.: We go back to sleep.

4:10 a.m.: Kelsey wants a drink of water.

4:14 a.m.: We go back to sleep.

5:00 a.m.: Anna's alarm goes off. She gets up to get ready for work.

5:45 a.m.: Claire screams. Anna gets Claire a bottle.

6:00 a.m.: Anna leaves for work. Sound of the front door shutting wakes all of the kids who scream for Mommy.

6:45 a.m.: Finally, get kids to lay back down.

6:46 a.m.: I lay back down.

7:00 a.m.: Alarm goes off.

7:03 a.m.: Get babies out of the cribs.

7:04 a.m.: Put bread in the toaster.

7:04 a.m.: Try to wake Kelsey.

7:05 a.m.: Make milk bottles for babies.

7:06 a.m.: Crack eggs into a bowl to make scrambled eggs.

7:06 a.m.: Toast pops.

7:06 a.m.: Emma bites Quinn over a toy.

7:07 a.m.: Give Emma a time-out.

7:08 a.m.: Try to wake Kelsey.

7:08 a.m.: Claire spills eggs on the floor, breaks the bowl.

7:09 a.m.: Clean up eggs and broken bowl.

7:09 a.m.: Get Quinn off the dining table.

7:09 a.m.: Get Emma off the dining table.

7:10 a.m.: Find Claire playing in the toilet.

7:11 a.m.: Clean up Claire.

7:11 a.m.: Get Quinn off the dining table.

7:11 a.m.: Get Emma off the dining table.

7:12 a.m.: Try to wake Kelsey.

7:13 a.m.: Discover Emma has spilled her milk bottle.

7:13 a.m.: Discover Quinn sitting in spilled milk. He is crying. I tell him not to cry over spilled milk.

7:14 a.m.: Change Quinn again.

7:16 a.m.: Get Claire off the dining table.

7:16 a.m.: Get Emma off the dining table.

7:17 a.m.: Babies start screaming for breakfast.

7:18 a.m.: Put babies in high chairs.

7:19 a.m.: Try to wake Kelsey.

7:20 a.m.: Try to butter toast; it's cold.

7:21 a.m.: Give babies Pop-Tarts. They throw them.

7:22 a.m.: Give babies a bowl of Cocoa Puffs.

7:22 a.m.: Tell babies to sit down in a high chair.

7:23 a.m.: Put bread in the toaster for me.

7:24 a.m.: Go to the bathroom.

7:25 a.m.: Try to wake Kelsey.

7:25 a.m.: My toast pops.

7:26 a.m.: Salesman calls. I threaten to kill him.

7:26 a.m.: Tell babies to sit down in a high chair.

7:26 a.m.: Claire dumps the soggy Cocoa Puffs on the floor.

7:26 a.m.: Tell babies to sit down in a high chair.

7:26 a.m.: Give Claire a Pop-Tart.

7:26 a.m.: Tell babies to sit down in a high chair.

7:28 a.m.: Claire is finished eating, throws Pop-Tart.

7:29 a.m.: Clean up earlier dumped Cocoa Puffs.

7:31 a.m.: Tell Quinn to sit down in a high chair.

7:31 a.m.: Try to wake Kelsey.

7:32 a.m.: Emma is finished eating, throws remaining Cocoa Puffs.

7:33 a.m.: Get Claire off the dining table.

7:33 a.m.: Get Emma off the dining table.

7:33 a.m.: Get Claire off the dining table again!

7:33 a.m.: Get Emma off the dining table again!

7:33 a.m.: Tell Quinn to sit down in a high chair.

7:34 a.m.: Anna calls to see if I'm awake yet! I tell her I am.

7:35 a.m.: Quinn is done with breakfast and wants down. He throws a bowl.

7:36 a.m.: Discover my toast is long cold.

7:37 a.m.: Eat my toast while I clean Emma's thrown Cocoa Puffs.

7:39 a.m.: Try to wake Kelsey.

7:40 a.m.: Change Emma's diaper.

7:42 a.m.: Change Quinn's diaper.

7:43 a.m.: Change Claire's diaper.

7:44 a.m.: Start the search for baby shoes.

7:45 a.m.: Turn on cartoons for babies.

7:47 a.m.: Try to wake Kelsey. Pick her up and put her on her feet. She appears to be up.

7:48 a.m.: Shave. (I'll shower tomorrow.)

7:52 a.m.: Try to wake Kelsey.

7:55 a.m.: Emma bites Quinn again.

7:56 a.m.: Comfort Quinn.

8:01 a.m.: Try to wake Kelsey.

8:03 a.m.: Give Emma a time-out.

8:04 a.m.: Find Claire and Quinn playing in the toilet.

8:05 a.m.: Give Claire and Quinn a bath. Emma wants one too.

8:15 a.m.: Baths over. Try to wake Kelsey.

8:17 a.m.: Put a new diaper on Quinn.

8:18 a.m.: Put a new diaper on Claire.

8:19 a.m.: Can't find Emma.

8:22 a.m.: Find Emma outside in the sandbox. Get Emma.

8:23 a.m.: Find Claire and Quinn playing in the toilet.

8:24 a.m.: Bang head on the wall.

8:25 a.m.: Give Claire and Quinn another bath.

8:40 a.m.: Baths over.

8:41 a.m.: Try to wake Kelsey. Put her in the bathtub! She wakes up, screaming that her pajamas are wet.

8:42 a.m.: Find Quinn's shoes in the trash can.

8:43 a.m.: Dress Kelsey. Can't find her socks.

8:50 a.m.: Discover babies have pulled every can out of the pantry cabinet.

8:51 a.m.: Find Claire's shoes in the pantry.

8:54 a.m.: Nanny calls asking why I'm late!

8:56 a.m.: Dress Claire.

9:00 a.m.: Can't find Emma.

9:00 a.m.: Can't find Kelsey.

9:00 a.m.: Can't find Quinn.

9:02 a.m.: Claire and I find them in the sandbox.

9:03 a.m.: Claire joins others in the sandbox.

9:04 a.m.: I run inside to find clothes for others.

9:10 a.m.: Finish gathering all needed clothes, shoes, and socks.

9:12 a.m.: Discover Kelsey has turned on a garden hose in the sandbox.

9:13 a.m.: Bang my head on an apple tree.

9:14 a.m.: Turn off the hose. Unscrew it from the faucet.

9:14 a.m.: Go inside to get new clothes for Kelsey and Claire.

9:18 a.m.: Return with more clothes.

9:20 a.m.: Redress Claire.

9:24 a.m.: Strap Claire in a car seat.

9:25 a.m.: Put in kids' music tape, start the car, turn on air conditioning.

9:26 a.m.: Give Claire a toy and open all car doors.

9:27 a.m.: Dress Quinn on the hood of the car.

9:34 a.m.: Strap Quinn in a car seat.

9:37 a.m.: Dress Emma on the hood of the car.

9:42 a.m.: Strap Emma in a car seat. Find Kelsey's shoes in the car.

9:44 a.m.: Snotty nanny calls again. She wants to know if I plan to bring the kids over any time soon.

9:47 a.m.: Dress Kelsey again.

9:55 a.m.: Strap Kelsey in a car seat.

9:57 a.m.: Run inside and grab my clothes.

10:02 a.m.: Dress myself by the hood of the car.

10:07 a.m.: Get in the car.

10:08 a.m.: Start driving.

10:15 a.m.: Return home to get Kelsey's lunch.

10:17 a.m.: Get in the car.

10:35 a.m.: Arrive at nanny's.

10:38 a.m.: Snotty nanny asks again why I'm so late.

10:44 a.m.: Get triplets inside nanny's house.

10:46 a.m.: Get in the car.

11:10 a.m.: Arrive at Kelsey's school.

11:13 a.m.: Get in the car.

11:30 a.m.: My class starts.

11:40 a.m.: I arrive at my classroom.

1:00 p.m.: My class ends.

1:10 p.m.: My next class starts.

3:00 p.m.: My class ends.

3:10 p.m.: Arrive at my office.

3:00 p.m.: Prepare for the next day's lessons.

4:00 p.m.: Pick up Kelsey at her school.

4:45 p.m.: Arrive at home.

4:45 p.m.: Pick up can goods from this morning.

4:49 p.m.: Start on breakfast dishes.

5:00 p.m.: Anna starts dinner.

5:02 p.m.: Babies and I watch cartoons.

5:25 p.m.: Dinner's ready.

5:32 p.m.: Get the last baby in a high chair.

5:45 p.m.: Babies are done eating and want out.

5:46 p.m.: Anna finally gets to sit down and eat.

5:47 p.m.: Claire wants in Anna's lap.

5:48 p.m.: Emma wants in Anna's lap.

5:49 p.m.: Quinn wants in Anna's lap.

5:50 p.m.: Anna gives up on dinner.

5:52 p.m.: I finish eating.

5:55 p.m.: We try to clear the table.

5:57 p.m.: Quinn dumps a plate full of food on the floor.

6:00 p.m.: Anna starts the babies' bath.

6:00 p.m.: I start cleaning dinner dishes.

6:30 p.m.: Baths are done.

6:33 p.m.: We diaper and put pajamas on babies.

7:00 p.m.: Make bottles for babies.
7:06 p.m.: Babies watch *Winnie the Pooh*.
8:00 p.m.: Put the babies in bed.
Repeat all of the above.

This Woman

∞∞∞

Still lost in the warped world that exists in the nadir of sleep and wake, I struggle to gain clarity, yet I'm already aware that something is wrong. I sense that missing from this process is the usual chaos of children demanding food or comfort and the need for me to wake instantaneously.

Disoriented and through foggy eyes, I watch a kaleidoscope of sunlight dance on a distant wall and obediently wait for the daze of dreams to cross-fade to the hard-edged focus required for thought. Then slowly, as if caught in a slow-motion movie, I turn to check the clock and stare as if a fog has hypnotized my view.

I am startled to reality as the clock blinks from 9:31 a.m. to 9:32 a.m. Confused and in disbelief, I paw at my eyes and quickly sit up. "This can't be right," I think to myself. "The kids are always awake by at least six thirty, certainly never later than seven." Checking my wrist for confirmation, I am suddenly terrified by unimaginable thoughts. I'm launched to my feet and sent banging into the bedroom door in a mad scramble to find my missing brood.

A bright, clear day throws golden light through the kids' window as I race to save my missing children. In a panic and ready to perform CPR, I check each bed only to find it empty. Horrified, I check under the beds and in closets, then run from room to room yelling like a madman in a desperate search for some hidden truth. Not finding them, I quickly grab the phone and started to dial.

Suddenly I hear giggling and the sound of snow pants and puffy fall clothing scraping against itself outside. I look out the window in time to see a cascade of leaves landing on top of a tangle of little arms and legs. Suddenly relaxed, I listen to the squeals and watch as the creator of this laughter smiles and glitters in the brisk fall air.

In the center of this action stands a woman, hair littered with broken leaves and cheeks pink from the frosty morning air. This woman has been hanging around our house. It is in this instant that I'm suddenly aware that she has actually been living in the house with us for quite a long time. She plays with the children, she cleans and cooks, and she does an awful lot of nice things for us. I appreciate all of the help that she gives us and all of the things that she does for us. I just don't know who she is. She reminds me of someone that I used to know. She is pretty in all the same ways as that person and even has the same laugh and the same smile. She looks at me like I know her, and I'm pretty sure that I should.

I've been so busy lately that, somehow, I've lost track of what she means to me. I always say hello to her, and we are always nice to each other. But it occurs to me that I've been so busy trying to survive the reality of life in this household that I don't talk to her very much. I don't know why. I feel silly, but it just never occurred to me to try to talk to her. We talk about the kids and what needs to get done and stuff like that, but we never speak with each other about other things, like each other.

Just yesterday morning, for example, I was walking down our hallway with an armful of toys. I had just picked them up, and she was walking in the other direction with an armful of baby shoes she had just picked up. For a brief second, we both stopped and looked at each other like we had something to say. I looked at her, and she looked at me, and then it struck me.

For the first time in three years, this woman and I were alone together. Completely alone. There were no babies as far as the eye could see. No one was screaming for toys or juice or due to the sudden lack of oxygen in their particular world. Neither of us was carrying a baby, changing a diaper, or cleaning up some disgusting spill, puke, or accident. We stood there, feeling goofy. She smiled that big beautiful smile of hers and disappeared down the hall in search of the kids.

I watch as the kids run around the yard, stopping only long enough to pull leaves off the tree and throw them in the air. I see her smile as she watches them dance and shriek in a swirl of floating leaves. She sees me watching her and throws a tiny wave my way as the kids grab her hands and lead her to the growing pile of crumpled brown leaves. She is quickly covered as the kids jump and roll around in the collection that includes their mom. She lifts her head and smiles again at me, then is soon snowed under by yet another wave of leaves. I think to myself that I should get to know this lady again.